Original title:
A Room of Roots

Copyright © 2025 Creative Arts Management OÜ
All rights reserved.

Author: Juliana Wentworth
ISBN HARDBACK: 978-1-80581-897-7
ISBN PAPERBACK: 978-1-80581-424-5
ISBN EBOOK: 978-1-80581-897-7

Echoing Through the Channels

In a house where whispers play,
Pineapple socks rule the day.
Dancing shadows on the floor,
Chasing echoes, wanting more.

Jelly beans in every nook,
A secret munching, come take a look.
Silly giggles, a falling shoe,
Who knew roots could throw a zoo?

Fragments of the Forgotten

Underneath the couch so bright,
Lost socks throwing quite a fright.
Scribbled notes from days of yore,
A rubber chicken at the door.

Dust bunnies doing the cha-cha,
Old toys dreaming of a gala.
Time forgot, but naps remain,
In corners, laughter's sweet refrain.

Canopy of Memories

Beneath the quilt, the stories lie,
Banana peels refuse to dry.
Tickle fights with dust and air,
While chairs hold secrets yet to share.

Marshmallow clouds on rainy days,
Hide and seek in funny ways.
Photos laughing from the shelf,
Remind us not to take ourselves.

Rhythms of the Underground

In the basement, boxes rust,
Socks and slippers formed a trust.
Party hats on every ghost,
Joking wildly, they make toast.

A carpet sip of grape juice fun,
Dance-offs with the washing machine spun.
Roots of laughter tangled deep,
Collecting dreams for us to keep.

Tethered to the Soil

In a patch where weeds play hide and seek,
The carrots giggle, 'We're far from meek!'
The radishes blush, all snug in the dark,
While potatoes plot a daring embark.

The tomatoes tease the witty old sage,
As they sway to the rhythms of age.
Onions laugh as they peel off a joke,
While garlic grins with each friendly poke.

Secrets of the Subterranean

Beneath the ground, where shadows prance,
Worms are ready for a wiggly dance.
Moles hum tunes in their tiny brigade,
While fungi throw a rave in the shade.

The roots exchange tips on how to grow tall,
While laughing at those who can't stand at all.
A beetroot's tales of muddy escapades,
Make the daisies snicker in leafy charades.

Life in the Loam

In the loam where the grubs have a feast,
Ants throw a party, to say the least!
With crumbs and bits, they dance and jig,
While beetles join in, each wearing a wig.

The snails slide in for a slow-motion race,
While crickets keep time with an upbeat pace.
And mushrooms, in hats, share the latest gossip,
As night falls down, they never stop this.

The Hidden Garden

Behind the walls where sunflowers snooze,
The strawberries chuckle in bright, berry hues.
With bees buzzing softly a sweet serenade,
The flowers are gossiping, oh, what a trade!

The garden gnome tells secrets in jest,
While ladybugs settle in for a rest.
The pumpkins are plotting a Halloween scheme,
In this hidden realm, life seems like a dream.

Fossils of Feeling

In the corner, a sock, alone,
Beneath a pile, its story's grown.
Could it be from a dinosaur's past?
Or just my laundry's strange contrast?

Dust bunnies dance like they're possessed,
Waging war on the sofa, no rest.
They cling to crumbs like they're gold coins,
Fossils of joy in my sock drawer's joins.

Echoes Underfoot

The floorboards creak like a giggling child,
Every step feels like a prank, so wild.
The echoes speak, they have much to say,
About all the snacks I've dropped in play.

Beneath the couch, a time machine,
Takes me back to snacks I've seen.
Echoes of laughter, crumbs galore,
My floor's a museum of munching lore.

The Trail Beneath

There's a trail of crumbs leading away,
A feast for ants, or a lunch gone astray?
With every step, the snack saga grows,
Leading to lost treasures, who knows?

I stumble over a rogue potato chip,
Could this be my adventurous trip?
Ants march on like tiny soldiers,
Gathering treasures on their shoulders.

Ties That Bind

Old shoelaces, tangled and frayed,
Binding my past in a playful parade.
Each knot tells a tale of its own,
Of misadventures in lands unknown.

They tie me to memories, oh so dense,
A trip to the park that seems too immense.
Yet in their chaos, a laughter shines,
Ties that bind in the quirkiest lines.

The Lies Beneath

Beneath the floor, things creep and crawl,
A sock, a shoe, and crumbs we sprawl.
The dust bunnies laugh, they hold a feast,
Funny how clutter becomes a beast.

In the corner, the laughter grows loud,
Old magazines form a paper crowd.
Tales of fashion that never took flight,
Mocking my choices, oh what a sight!

Shadows of the Undergrowth

In shadows deep where secrets lie,
An old broomstick waves goodbye.
It swears it's a wizard, ready to play,
But all it does is gather clay.

A plant on the shelf, with a leafy grin,
Says, "I'm the king, let the fun begin!"
Yet every morning, it droops and sighs,
When the sunlight peeks, oh what a surprise!

Growth and Gravity

Oh, the weight of my snacks does grow,
As I sit on this chair, no need to show.
Gravity's pull on my snack-filled lap,
Causes giggles, a laughter trap!

A sprout on the sill, in yoga pose,
Pretends to stretch while I doze.
It thinks it's wise, oh what a shame,
Can't even tell it's in the same game!

Interwoven Histories

In this space where tales entwine,
Old photos wink, they sip their wine.
They gossip sweetly about the past,
As I trip over memories, but what a blast!

The wallpaper's peeling, but don't you fret,
It's a mural of chaos, my favorite bet.
Each crack a story, each tear a jest,
In this hodgepodge room, I'm truly blessed!

The Heart of the Earth

Beneath the ground, where giggles hide,
Worms throw parties, roots abide.
Moles are DJs, spinning tunes,
While grasses dance beneath the moons.

Bubbles rise from marshy glee,
Tadpoles sing in jubilee.
The soil laughs with earthy jokes,
As toadstools play the funny folks.

Beneath the Surface

In underground lanes, there's a show,
Rabbits wearing hats say, "Hello!"
They're planning picnics near the ferns,
Where dancing beetles take their turns.

Rooty friends, all intertwined,
Share their snacks, like vines combined.
Nuts are jokes, and leaves are cheers,
As old oak trees lend them their ears.

Echoes of the Ancients

Hidden whispers of laughter gleam,
Ancient roots with a playful dream.
Squirrels clutch their acorn charms,
While vines weave tales in leafy arms.

Ghosts of plants in flamboyant styles,
Make faces from their earthen piles.
Their echoes ripple within the earth,
Creating giggles, giving birth.

Gnarled Memories

Knotted tales in bark unfold,
Of wacky roots, a sight to behold.
Compost critters crack a jest,
While elder branches know the best.

Beneath the chaos, chaos sleeps,
With weed jokes that make everyone weep.
Gnarled memories, twisted yarns,
Fluffy moss in mischievous barns.

The Network Below

Beneath the floor, they wiggle and weave,
A secret society, you won't believe!
They gossip and giggle, share tales of the dirt,
While nibbling on crumbs, oh what a flirt!

Roots tangled in mischief, a party unseen,
Trading some gossip, like it's a routine.
'You call that a branch? Oh, please take a seat,
I've seen twigs more charming with roots under feet!'

Grounded Dreams

In dreams, I'm sprouting, the height of a tree,
With leaves made of bubbles, oh what glee!
Each branch a wild story, each root a big laugh,
I'm the tallest of veggies—check out my staff!

The whispers of radishes tickle my ears,
Saying, 'Make room for carrots, we're conquering fears!'
A parade in the soil, where the worms have a ball,
They're spinning and dancing, who's the root of it all?

The Soul of the Subsoil

Down in the depths where the shadows play,
The roots throw a party at the end of the day.
They sip on the moisture, a drink quite divine,
And toast to the worms who've been working on time.

With laughter in layers, they tease and they jest,
Claiming they know who's the very best dressed.
'I'm wearing compost, and you're sporting clay,
We're the root trendsetters, leading the way!'

Garden of Echoes

In the garden of giggles, we plant all our dreams,
With echoes of laughter bursting at the seams.
Each seed is a joke, just waiting to sprout,
When flowers start blooming, there's no room for doubt!

The daisies are chuckling, while petunias prance,
They're doing a jig as the weeds steal a glance.
In the soil of humor, they all take their turn,
Sharing their secrets, it's our time to learn!

Grounded Harmonies

In the corner, a plant starts to sway,
Making fun of the dust bunnies' play.
A cactus sports shades, feeling so cool,
While the fern rolls its eyes, calls it a fool.

The pot sits proudly, a throne for the leaf,
Whispering tales of absurd disbelief.
A spider spins webs, glimmers of glee,
Says, "Life's a big party, come dance here with me!"

The soil below is a giggling mass,
Throwing jokes at the roots as they pass.
With each little sprout, laughter does grow,
In this wacky abode, there's always a show.

So next time you wander past that old vine,
Remember its humor – it's quite divine!
Roots may be grounded, yet spirits can fly,
In this quirky realm, we all laugh and sigh.

Soil's Subtle Secrets

The earth chuckles softly, whispers its creed,
In the depths of the garden, joy's all we need.
Worms hold a conference, in suits made of dirt,
Discussing the merits of squiggle and spurt.

A mole's got a hat, it's quite a surprise,
He digs little tunnels and wears tiny ties.
With a wink and a nod, he burrows with style,
Saying, "I'm just a groundhog, working my pile!"

The flowers, they gossip, comparing their blooms,
"Oh darling, you're stunning, like colorful plumes!"
They dance in the breeze, a fabulous crew,
Mixing laughter and petals, in colors so true.

The sun peeks through branches, a warm smile at play,
Inviting us all to join in the fray.
So gather 'round friends, in this silly soirée,
Where roots hold the punchlines, and laughter's our tray!

Foundations of Being

In the basement of existence, we reside,
Where odd socks and lost dreams collide.
A cat with a hat, it's quite a sight,
Whiskered philosopher pondering at night.

The floorboards creak in a jazzy tune,
Telling secrets to the glow of the moon.
A rubber plant waltzes, oh what a spree,
While dust bunnies giggle, 'Come dance with me!'

Pots of spaghetti hang from the ceiling,
Noodles 'n' laughter, oh what a feeling!
Cousins of chaos, we all must admit,
In this silly abode, life's a wild skit.

So let's raise a toast to the roots down low,
To the funny little things that make life glow.
With a chuckle or two and a wink at fate,
We're all just vines tangled, isn't it great?

Nature's Embrace

In the garden of giggles, shrubs sway in rhyme,
A mouse in a tutu, perfectly in time.
The daisies are gossiping, giving a poke,
While gophers play poker, sharing some smoke.

A squirrel with a mustache steals acorns from beds,
While the roses are chatting about their love spreads.
The wind whispers jokes to the trees standing tall,
As crickets compose symphonies, holding their call.

Oh, Mother Nature, the prankster divine,
Bringing laughter through blossoms and goofy design.
With each chuckling leaf, and each fluttering wing,
You remind us of joy in the madness we bring.

So here's to the laughter in petals and dirt,
To the fun in the fields and the world's little quirks.
For in every garden where the silly sun plays,
We find roots of humor brightening our days!

The Underground Symphony

Beneath the surface where shadows delight,
A beetle conducts an orchestra of night.
With the thump of a worm and a flutter of wings,
They play at the beat of the earth's silly flings.

A concert of giggles, and laughter so bold,
The gophers tap dance on stories untold.
With every deep note, and every soft sigh,
The roots join in harmony, lifting up high.

A mischievous mole shouts, 'Let's jam till we drop!'
While earthworms boogie, they just can't stop.
The twinkle of soil, in its earthy embrace,
Transforms into music, a rhythmic showcase.

So whisper your secrets beneath leafy crowns,
Join the wild symphony of our underground towns.
Feel the joy rising up from below to the sky,
In this funny ballet, let your spirits fly!

Depths of Discovery

In the wild of the world, where the laughter is vast,
We dig for the treasures, not shadows we cast.
With spades of absurdity, we unearth delight,
Finding socks, old toys, and a sparkly fright.

Each inch we explore is a journey of fun,
With roots tickling toes and a race just begun.
The garden of giggles, where oddities bloom,
Is a maze of reminders of joy we consume.

What's that in the corner? A jellybean jar!
Filled with wishes and dreams we've piled up so far.
In the depths of discovery, we stumble today,
On the funny little things that come out to play.

So let's dig together, make a ruckus and cheer,
For life's little treasures are buried so near.
With laughter as our compass, we'll wander and roam,
In the depths of absurdity, we'll find our new home!

Threads of Heritage

In the attic, grandpa's hat,
Worn by squirrels, just like that.
A ghost of choices, full of glee,
Tangled yarns of my family tree.

The stories twist and pull me tight,
Grandma's dances in candlelight.
A sock of woes, that bears a hole,
Yet laughs remind me they're still whole.

A cousin's fable, funny and tall,
In homemade sweaters, we stand tall.
The bickering over who's the best,
In this woven chaos, I feel blessed.

So here's to threads that bind us well,
In every laugh, there's a tale to tell.
We may trip over roots now and then,
But laughter lifts us time and again.

Nestled in the Soil's Embrace

In the garden, worms tell jokes,
They wiggle 'round like little folks.
Roots wave hands, they dance and sway,
Underneath the moles' cabaret.

A carrot's sunbath, what a sight,
With goggly eyes, it's quite a fright.
Tomatoes giggle when they're crushed,
In this dirt party, hilarity's hushed.

A weed throws shade, feeling bold,
With dreams of growing, oh so old.
The flowers chuckle at faux pas,
As bees buzz in with laughter's law.

So plant your roots and sow some cheer,
Each laugh a seed, let joy appear.
In this earthy rumble, take your stance,
For life's a garden, so let's dance.

The Hidden Tapestry

Behind the wall, I heard a sound,
A tapestry that twirls around.
With threads of humor, stitched with care,
It patterns life in laughter's flare.

Grandma's secrets and Uncle Joe,
A blend of mischief in every row.
Snaps of whimsy, stories they tell,
In this vibrant weave, we frolic well.

A tapestry grows with funny threads,
Each stitch a giggle, no need for dreads.
A patchwork heart, snug and tight,
The quirk of life is pure delight.

So hang this fabric, bright and bold,
An art of roots, with stories told.
In every flicker, every gleam,
Laughter's echo shall redeem.

Memories in the Mould

In dusty corners, memories dwell,
Each speck of mould, a story to tell.
A pizza slice from '84,
That's definitely rooted in folklore.

The chairs all creak with elders' tales,
Of treasure hunts and pirate gales.
Chipped mugs grin in the kitchen light,
Cups of laughter, oh what a sight!

A jigsaw of forgotten games,
With missing pieces and funny names.
The walls hold echoes of our fun,
In this space, we've just begun.

So here's to mould, so full of charm,
A fuzzy friend, with no alarm.
In every corner, we find a grin,
For memories bloom where laughter's been.

Tendrils of Time

In a corner, a sock's gone rogue,
Tangled in memories like a stubborn fog.
Dust bunnies dance with a mischievous glee,
While the clock ticks loudly, just to tease me.

Old chairs creak, sharing secrets in style,
Of epic battles and a long lost smile.
The calendar's shocked, 'Is it December again?'
As the cat takes a nap, plotting world domination then.

Wires twist like spaghetti, a tech-locked embrace,
While snacks hide in cushions, a treasure to chase.
Time plays tricks, like a prankster friend,
Every wrinkle a story, never truly ends.

So let's laugh at the quirks, let mishaps unfold,
In a space full of laughter, let the truth be retold.
For the roots might be tangled, but joy is the vine,
In this chaotic abode, everything's fine.

Whispers in the Dark

The light flickers, but don't you fret,
The ghost of snack time is not gone yet.
A creak on the floor makes the heart race,
But it's just old Mr. Couch in his favorite place.

Walls have ears and they gossip and sigh,
'Is it snack o'clock? Oh my, oh my!'
The mice throw parties unseen by our eyes,
While shadows form lines, dancing 'neath the skies.

In the dead of the night, there's a thump and a plop,
It seems the cat's taken a very quick hop.
Jokes echo softly, like whispers on air,
In the quarters of chaos, we laugh without care.

So let's embrace the weird, the odd, and the crass,
In the silence of darkness, we'll cheerfully pass.
For even in shadows, laughter takes flight,
Turning mystery into a comedy night.

Pulse of the Earth

Beneath the floorboards, life's brewing a stew,
In the realm of the weird, where monsters are few.
Comedy's lurking in cracks of the ground,
With roots playing tag, making silly sounds.

The walls hum a tune, a jolly old song,
As ants march in line, feeling proud and strong.
Each wiggle of earth brings a chuckle and cheer,
Though no one can hear, we've got quite a seer.

Old boxes are portals to worlds worn and torn,
Filled with treasures, like the day I was born.
With every rumble, the house gives a grin,
As it shakes off the cobwebs of life once again.

So let's stomp our feet, shake out our roots,
In a place where the laughter and silliness hoots.
The earth's pulse a melody, a whimsical beat,
Where humor and joy always meet.

Anchored to the Past

Socks in the sofa, a misfit parade,
Gathering stories of yesterdays made.
In the mess of the memories, joy's never far,
Like lost treasures found in a crumb-eating jar.

The fridge whispers secrets, oh what a delight,
Leftovers argue, 'Who's going to take flight?'
Moldy cheese thinks it's the life of the show,
While expired mustard just wants to glow.

Pictures hang crooked, each one with a tale,
Of family antics, where laughter sets sail.
In corners of chaos, we find our old friends,
Through giggles and gaffes, the harmony blends.

So here's to the mishaps that make our days bright,
In a space steeped in history, we laugh with all might.
For anchored in memories, we're never alone,
In this home full of quirks, the laughter has grown.

Whispers Beneath the Floorboards

In shadows deep, the critters play,
Squeaky voices have their say.
A mouse in boots, a rat in cap,
They dance and sing, and take a nap.

The floorboards squeak, a giggling cheer,
They plan a party, oh my dear!
With crumbs and cheese as their fine feast,
The laughter grows, not yet the least.

A parrot tells a joke so fine,
While spiders weave with quirky line.
The dust bunnies roll, a silly sight,
While shadows sway, they take to flight.

So if you hear those whispers call,
Just know they're having a grand ball.
Join in the fun, don't be shy,
For life's a giggle, oh my my!

The Tangle of Ancestors

Up in the attic, a hat does spin,
An old shoe laughs, with a cheeky grin.
Grandpa's voice from a dusty box,
He cracks a joke that really rocks.

A tangled web of stories' thread,
With splendid yarns that seldom spread.
A family tree, oh what a sight,
Where branches wiggle with sheer delight.

A great-aunt's dress takes a dizzy twirl,
While uncles jive with an endless whirl.
The furniture shakes in riotous fun,
Where giggles echo when the day is done.

So listen close to the tales they share,
In tattered clothes, with laughter rare.
Each rusty clue, a memory bright,
In the tangled past, they take flight.

Secrets in the Sap

In the garden, the saplings dream,
Whispering secrets in chirpy gleam.
A squirrel spills the beans with glee,
About the roots beneath the tree.

"Oh, did you hear?" the daisies tease,
"The carrots dance in the evening breeze!"
Worms in wigs wiggle to the sound,
Making mischief beneath the ground.

A secret party of the soil's kin,
Where laughter bubbles up from within.
The thumping roots play hide and seek,
While flowers chatter, their voices peak.

So bend down low, it's quite a show,
With giggles sprouting, row by row.
The garden's heartbeat, a joyful blast,
In the sap, the future's cast!

Echoes of the Earth Below

Down below, the critters bicker,
With tiny voices, loud and snicker.
A gopher hums a goofy tune,
While crickets chirp beneath the moon.

The roots are tangled in playful knot,
Where laughter lives, and sadness not.
A chanting rhythm, thump and thud,
As they stomp around in happy mud.

"Bring on the fun! It's party time!"
Yells the hedgehog, quite sublime.
With nuts and twigs, they set the stage,
Each little critter, full of rage.

So if you hear an echo rise,
From deep within, it's no surprise.
The earth is tickled, beneath the ground,
With secrets shared, joy all around!

The Heart of the Foundation

In a house so deep with cheer,
Roots are giggling down there,
They tell jokes to the floor,
While the ceiling tries to ignore.

The walls hum tunes of the past,
As the furniture shakes and laughs,
A lamp wiggles with delight,
While shadows dance in the night.

Laughter travels up and around,
Tickling every heart it's found,
Chairs grow legs to skip and sway,
As sunlight steals the show each day.

In this place, the fun won't stop,
Roots lead a party, hop, hop, hop!
A comedy of nature sprouted,
Where roots and laughter are shouted!

Climbing Beyond the Canopy

Up I go, through towering greens,
Where roots conspire with comedy scenes,
They tickle the bark and tease the leaves,
For every branch, a giggle weaves.

Squirrels jest in acorn attire,
While birds join, raising the bar higher,
A chorus sings with each gentle sway,
As the sun peeks in to play.

I reach the top, feeling quite free,
A jesting breeze plays tricks on me,
Leaves rustle, whispering secrets true,
While roots cheer on, "We're proud of you!"

From high above, the world seems bright,
With roots below adding delight,
Every twist and every climb,
Is a punchline in nature's rhyme!

Echoing in Our Bones

In the base of our beings it spreads,
A melody of roots in our heads,
As laughter echoes through every twist,
Join the dance, it can't be missed!

Beneath the skin, the chuckles flow,
Roots that giggle, don't you know?
They pulse with joy, they jump and jive,
In this funny tune, we come alive!

Each heartbeat sings of roots so grand,
With each beat, the humor expands,
Glued together with roots embraced,
In the core of laughter we've traced.

So let your spirit wiggle and twine,
For in our bones, the roots intertwine,
Echoing jokes of the past and present,
Making sweet memories that are truly pleasant!

Grounded in Legacy

Here we stand, the roots of our past,
With a legacy built to last,
Each root a story, twisting with glee,
Making sure we always see.

Grandma's joke, a classic now,
Roots remember, "What's that?" "Wow!"
Dig deeper and you just might find,
A punchline crafted by nature's mind.

In the soil, history's embrace,
A comical tale of this place,
With roots that chuckle at every bend,
Creating a legacy that will never end!

So laugh with your roots, let them show,
The fun in the time we call 'below,'
Grounded in joy, the stories twine,
Each one a marker that's simply divine!

Tales from the Timberline

In a treehouse high, squirrels play,
They swipe my snacks and run away.
Raccoons throw parties with their cheer,
While owls hoot loudly, "We've got beer!"

A woodpecker drums like it's a band,
As chipmunks dance, quite unplanned.
A wise old tortoise calls the shots,
And all the critters roast their pots.

The breeze brings whispers through the leaves,
"Who stole my nuts?" a squirrel grieves.
The trees are gossiping, oh what fun,
While the sun peeks out, "Let's burn, everyone!"

So here I sit, beneath a pie,
Eating my shade, oh me, oh my!
In timber's tales, a laugh I find,
Nature's humor, oh so unconfined.

The Weight of the Undergrowth

Where underbrush stretches, a rabbit creeps,
With lettuce dreams, it hardly sleeps.
But roots trip flowers, oh what a mess,
As daisies complain, "We're under-dressed!"

A snail races but moves very slow,
Yelling, "Help! I've lost my home, oh no!"
The mushrooms giggle, "Look at that guy,
Running so fast but he'll never fly!"

The weevils plot a dance-off feast,
Competing for crumbs, to say the least.
While ants march on with a drumline sound,
Under zany laughter, the ground spins round.

In undergrowth thick, the humor grows,
Each leaf and twig has tales to disclose.
Mirth in the muck, where chaos thrives,
Among the roots, the comedy survives.

Beneath Branches and Beams

Beneath the branches, a jester squirrel,
Performs his tricks with a somersault whirl.
"Who needs a stage?" he declares with glee,
When a crowd of bugs pays to see!

A frog plays the trumpet, made of a leaf,
While passing beetles add to the beef.
Each critter nods, thinking it wise,
In this leafy hall, laughter's the prize.

A chorus of crickets starts a debate,
On who is the fittest, oh, isn't that great?
The wise old owl snores loud through the night,
While beetles round out with a late-night bite.

So sit a while in this leafy space,
With humor that's anchored and no hard case.
Above the beams, the antics beam,
Where nature's laughter reigns supreme.

The Tapestry of Earth

In the soil's weave, a worm takes a stand,
Saying, "Look at me, I'm quite grand!
With dinner at hand, I wiggle about,
Planet's clean-up crew, without a doubt!"

While daisies gossip, unfolding their charms,
Beetles roll by without any qualms.
"Did you hear the one 'bout the ant and the grass?"
Roars the hedgehog, oh what a class!

Tangled with roots, the laughter ensues,
As critters swap tales of their wild views.
Under the sun, they all gather 'round,
For jesters of nature, the joy is profound.

Thus in the ground, a comedy thrives,
The tapestry glimmers, proves life survives.
Nurtured in humor, where laughter's worth,
Together we share, this fun on Earth.

Subterranean Stories

Down in the soil, where the worms spin tales,
The gnomes hold court in their mossy veils.
With cups of tea made from dew-drenched grass,
They gossip about the leaves that pass.

Rabbits waltzing with the sneaky old mole,
Claiming high scores on the fat carrot roll.
They laugh and cheer, what a muddy affair,
While roots play leapfrog in the cool, damp air.

Fungi bust out in their vibrant attire,
Organizing dances that never expire.
They spin and twirl, with a laugh and a jig,
While shadows of beetles play hide and seek big.

So next time you walk on a sidewalk bright,
Remember the tales that dance out of sight.
For down below, where the bumps are quite funny,
Lies a kingdom of laughter, not just soil and honey.

The Cradle of Creation

In a cozy nook where the sun shines low,
The sleepers, the dreamers, the roots start to grow.
They plot and they scheme, in whispers they share,
Ideas that tangle as they twist through the air.

A seedling once sneezed, and the whole garden shook,
The plants all erupted, inspiration they took.
With rhymes in their leaves, they held a grand meet,
To brainstorm new ways to grow fancy and neat.

With cacti recounting their tales of the sun,
And violets giggling, just having some fun.
They painted the night with their colorful glows,
While twigs tapped the rhythm of roots in their throes.

Oh what a sight, this creation's delight,
With stories and laughter weaving through the night.
Each sprout tells a tale, each petal a song,
In the cradle of mirth, where all folks belong.

Roots of Reflection

Hidden below where the secrets reside,
The roots hold a mirror, reflecting our pride.
They chuckle and snicker at things we think grand,
Concealing our worries in their slender band.

They're wise in their ways, these underground friends,
Pondering life while the sunlight descends.
A tuber once joked, 'I'm the real superstar,
In the world above, they just don't know who we are!'

A giddy old root smiled, 'Come hear our tales,
The times of the wind and the rainy gales.'
With laughter they spun through the face of the earth,
While creatures above sang their praise and mirth.

So if you should find a root peeking through,
Remember it's simply a peek into you.
With wiggles and giggles, they spread like a cheer,
Enlightening the world to the joys down here.

The Depths Speak

Gather 'round, friends, as the depths start to chat,
With whispers of mushrooms and a wise old bat.
They gossip about the grass tickling their toes,
As adventurers wander above, who knows?

The roaches hold meetings on what to disguise,
While snails slide on by with their intricate lies.
'The leaf fell right here,' one old root said with glee,
'It's the best gossip-spree that you'll ever see!'

Jellybeans tumble from the ground's playful cheer,
Surprising the critters that gather quite near.
A celebration's brewing, so join in the fun,
As laughter erupts 'neath the warm shining sun.

So let not the world beyond ever forget,
The party below, where the laughs are well-met.
For buried in soil, with spirits so spry,
The depths laugh together while the surface says hi.

Hidden Heritage

In the attic, old shoes wail,
Worn by a ghost with a tale.
They shuffle and giggle, we laugh,
Chasing echoes of a forgotten path.

Dust bunnies form a parade,
With each tiny hop, a charade.
They lead to treasures unseen,
Like grandma's pants with a rich beet sheen.

Under the floorboards, whispers play,
Uncle Joe's socks from yesterday.
They clamor, they cluck, a fashion show,
Is this the hidden style we know?

Roots of laughter take their stance,
As all the memories start to dance.
So next time you find an old boot,
Remember the joy it bears, pink and cute!

Entwinement

The cat and the plant, in a snit,
Curled together, isn't that a hit?
They scheme and conspire, what a laugh,
Plotting pranks for the lazy giraffe.

Vines creeping on the couch, oh dear,
They've made a home where it's unclear.
The sofa's lost in a leaf buffet,
And so has the remote, hideaway!

Chairs biting chairs in a cheeky fight,
A brawl that lasted well through the night.
Who knew wood was so prone to flair?
Entwined in antics, a furniture affair!

As roots and legs join in the fun,
You'd think they ran a marathon!
If laughter's a plant, we've sown a tree,
With sitting roots, happy as can be!

Stories in the Soil

The pot has secrets, deep and wide,
With each sprout, a story to bide.
Worms in suits share their grand lore,
Of the times they slithered and explored.

Moles in hats, planning their plot,
To surprise the garden, but forgot!
They giggle as they dig and dive,
Telling tales of how to thrive.

The daisies gossip, petals aflutter,
Over dirt donuts they giggle and mutter.
"Did you hear about the old tree's sway?
It danced with the breeze, hip-hip-hooray!"

Every inch of loam holds a jest,
Nurturing laughter, it's simply the best.
So when you dig down, give a grin,
For the tales from the earth are sure to win!

Firmament of Roots

Up in the attic, where shadows play,
Lies a root party on grand display.
With limbs for limbs and laughter as fuel,
Who knew that a vine could be so cool?

Skyward they reach, twirling about,
"Catch us if you can!" they shout.
Up the walls, down the hall,
These roots aren't shy; they're having a ball!

Squirrels in tuxedos, with acorns to share,
Crash the soirée, without a care.
They leap and they dance, with roots in tow,
Creating a ruckus, a fabulous show.

In this upper realm, where laughter sprout,
A firmament of fun, there's no doubt.
So if you wander where the roots zoom,
Join the gala, find your groove in the bloom!

Roots and Reveries

In the corner lurks a plant,
With thoughts that make it rant.
It dreams of shoes and hats,
And chatting with the cats.

Leaves shaking with delight,
They spread their tales at night.
What if I could dance,
And wear a leafy pants?

A tangle here, a twist there,
The neighbors stop and stare.
I swear they have a plot,
To grow a dancing lot!

Their laughter fills the air,
Roots whisper everywhere.
In our little leafy show,
Who needs sunlight to grow?

Veins of the Wilderness

In the wild, the roots conspire,
Plotting mischief, never tire.
A berry claims a throne,
While thorns throw sticks and stones.

Squirrels hold a mock debate,
On who gets the bigger plate.
Acorns roll, laughter grows,
As the mushrooms strike a pose.

The flowers chuckle, gossip spree,
"Did you see what grew from me?"
Budding friendships bloom so bright,
While weeds laugh at llama fright.

Roots are busy, crafty pals,
Pulling tricks on passing gals.
They flip-flop, twirl, then freeze,
Grinning at the busy bees.

Underworld Melodies

Beneath the ground, a band does play,
With rooty tunes to save the day.
They strum on rocks, beat on mud,
Their rhythms thump with silly thud.

A carrot sings in joyful glee,
While mushrooms join, "Oh, dance with me!"
The underground has quite the show,
Twinkle-toes in dirt, you know.

Dandelions sway and sway,
As radishes lead the ballet.
The soil boogies, quite absurd,
As worms shout, "We're never heard!"

The laughter bubbles from below,
As roots drop beats, the veggies flow.
Could this be the next big hit?
In nature's club, we don't quit!

Life's Silent Support

Roots have secrets, wise and deep,
With laughs that never let us sleep.
On quiet nights, they joke and creep,
Whispering tales while we just peep.

They hold us up, that's their game,
Yet sometimes, it feels quite lame.
"Feed us more," the blossoms plead,
While roots just laugh, "You're a weed!"

In silence, they scheme and plot,
Whispers shared in the garden lot.
"Who's the tallest? Who's the best?"
Roots giggle, "We'll take the rest!"

So here's to roots, those jokesters sly,
Supporting life while we just sigh.
In every twist, they find their cheer,
Our silent friends, always near!

Shadows of the Forgotten

In corners where dust bunnies play,
Old memories hide, in a silly way.
A sock on the ceiling, it swings with glee,
Is that a ghost or just a lost key?

The cat leaps high, her antics a show,
Chasing phantoms only she knows.
Laughter erupts as the shadows loom,
Who knew past quirks could brighten a room?

Creaking floors join in the fun,
Squeaky shoes? Oh, what a run!
A mirror reflects a grin so wide,
Echoes of laughter, our silly guide.

In the back, a pile of old clothes,
Stand like soldiers in mismatched rows.
They giggle as we rummage around,
In this odd space, smiles abound.

Lifelines of the Living

Beneath the table, a monster resides,
A dust bunny army, where chaos abides.
With snacks on the floor, a feast has begun,
In this land of crumbs, we're all having fun.

Plants in the corner, they sway with grace,
Whispering secrets in this playful place.
A cactus jokes, "I'm prickly, it's true,
But my friends are all rooting for me and you!"

A light bulb flickers, a fixture of cheer,
Every glitch tells a joke, loud and clear.
We cheer for the bugs that dance on the wall,
In our lively embrace, we're having a ball!

Life sprawls around in colors so bright,
As laughter and love fill the quirky night.
Each echo of joy, a lifeline we share,
In this cheerful circus, we breathe the sweet air.

Beneath the Surface

Underneath the bed, a shoe thief dwells,
In a realm of odd smells and hidden spells.
That old dust sock, with its glorious fate,
Lives a grand life of whims, can't hesitate!

The rug sings secrets of journeys long past,
Spinning fibs of who's lost, who's fast.
Coffee stains narrate a tale of delight,
And crumbs keep the laughter alive every night.

Beneath the surface of everyday trials,
Laughter bubbles up in unexpected styles.
A tablecloth flaps like a flag unfurled,
Saying, "Join the party, come give it a whirl!"

Under the surface lies a treasure trove,
Of stories that tease and the memories rove.
As we dance 'round the room, a silly parade,
In this hidden realm, our joy is displayed.

Interwoven Histories

In our realm of woven tales and threads,
Mismatched socks socialize, lose their dreads.
A blanket fort stands like a castle grand,
With silly rules only we understand.

The wallpaper peeks, like a curious spy,
Listening closely to every joke and sigh.
When walls could talk, oh, the tales they'd tell,
Of giggles and grumbles that broke every spell.

Tangled roots hold hands with the fun,
Each knot tells stories of everyone.
A quirky team of relics and glee,
Creating a tapestry just for you and me.

And in this space where laughter sprouts,
Each history woven makes our joy shout.
So let's celebrate all the quirks that we bring,
In this wild interlace, let our laughter sing!

The Nest of Time

In a corner, dust bunnies play,
Whispering secrets of yesterday.
Clocks tick tock in a silly race,
While socks try to find their place.

Each tick a giggle, each tock a cheer,
As the couch cushions plot their career.
Pillows are judges; they hold a court,
With blankets and sheets as their support.

When shoes start dancing, oh what a sight,
As the cat joins in with sheer delight.
Time bows out, with a wink and a grin,
Saying, "Maybe I'll come back again!"

Buried Voices

Underneath the cluttered heap,
Dusty shoes and secrets creep.
Whispers come from old pizza boxes,
Joking about their past bedrock processes.

The monsters under the bed snicker,
As the socks reveal a giggly kicker.
"To the laundry!" they shout with glee,
As the lost change laughs, "Look at me!"

Canned beans form a conga line,
While pop cans bubble; oh so fine!
Voices chuckle, forgotten in the shade,
Buried treasures in a joy parade.

Entwined Echoes

Echoes bounce off the peeling wall,
Sneaking laughs from a two-footed thrall.
A painting grimaces, eyes wide and bright,
As the floor creaks at the ghostly fight.

The rug rebels, a soft little prank,
While the chair attempts to form a rank.
Dancing forks from the drawer brigade,
Making music as they serenade.

"Mismatched spoons unite!" they declare,
In a feast of laughter, joy fills the air.
Entwined tales woven with joy and cheer,
As the very walls shout, "Stay here, stay here!"

Where Life Intersects

Where the clothes meet and chaos reigns,
A rubber duck floats in the drains.
Loved socks mingle with abandoned keys,
Fluffy winter hats sneeze in the breeze.

Ordinary objects have grand affairs,
With old comics and mismatched chairs.
They spin stories of laughter and fun,
While pondering where all the spoons run.

Busy lives crossing, a playful blend,
Of lost remote controls and playtime pretend.
In this silly space, they twist and shout,
Where life intersects, there's joy throughout.

Birthplace of Shadows

In a corner where whispers tease,
Laughter hides among the leaves.
A chair that squeaks like a mouse,
Claiming it's the heart of the house.

Potted plants wearing old hats,
Dancing to songs of chubby cats.
A sofa that swallows lost keys,
While dust bunnies giggle with ease.

Cobwebs knit with quite a flair,
Spiders hosting a fashion affair.
The shadows weave tales of their own,
In this charming little home.

Who knew a nook could contain so much?
With plants and critters, and chairs that clutch.
In corners where laughter's a shield,
A sanctuary only ghouls would yield.

The Quiet Below

Beneath the stairs lurks a fairytale,
With monsters whose socks tell a tale.
A vacuum waits, plotting its spree,
Declaring war on dust bunnies, whee!

An old trunk sings of quests untamed,
With treasures forgotten, yet untamed.
The quiet hums with secrets near,
And giggles coax out every dear.

Squeaky boots on the wooden floor,
Join in the fun, as boots explore.
The space alive with echoes bright,
Whispering jokes into the night.

A cluttered charm that steals the show,
A sanctuary that's ever aglow.
In shadows and laughter, we play the part,
In the quiet below, we find our heart.

Resonance of Roots

Beneath the floor lies a world of cheer,
With worms that disco and soil that's dear.
Crickets compose symphonies loud,
As the flowers sway, proud in their shroud.

With each tap, echoes lead the way,
To bugs in tuxedos at a fine soiree.
Chairs creak in rhythm, like a dance,
Bidding the creatures to take a chance.

The laughter rolls like thunder's tease,
As squirrels gather leaves with ease.
Roots that tangle and twist just right,
Hosting a party each starry night.

In this garden deep below,
Nature's whimsy tends to grow.
Veins of life hum in giggling tones,
A space alive, where laughter roams.

Pathways to the Past

In the attic where old dreams lie,
Monkeys play chess and owls fly.
Boxes stacked like stories tall,
Every whisper is a giggling call.

A mirror reflects the quirks of time,
Showing faces with a jester's rhyme.
Each artifact holds a tale or two,
Of silly moments we once knew.

Under the rug, a trapdoor waits,
With scribbled notes on forgotten plates.
Ghosts of giggles skip through the air,
Poking fun at those unaware.

Paths of laughter lead us back,
To stories hidden in the cracks.
With each adventure, joy will last,
In the pathways where shadows cast.

Threads Through the Earth

Beneath the floor, a party's set,
With dancing plants, they won't forget.
A rhubarb wears a polka dot,
While carrots sip from a teapot.

The radish laughs, a jolly round,
His leafy friends all gather 'round.
They sing of dirt and sunny days,
In root ballet, in funny ways.

A worm joins in, a wriggly chap,
With tiny moves, he takes a lap.
The broccoli twirls, it's quite a sight,
In this underground delight, oh what a night!

As overgrowth starts to intrude,
The roots just laugh, they won't be rude.
They know the fun is just begun,
In squishy soil, they'll always run.

Quietly Intertwined

In quiet corners, roots do play,
They whisper jokes in subtle ways.
The timid thyme giggles in the shade,
While mushrooms toss a wild charade.

A beetroot rolls, with quite a flair,
It spins and laughs, without a care.
With every twist, the vines pull tight,
Their tangled dance brings sheer delight.

The chives, they snicker, a snappy crew,
With witty banter, they join the stew.
In silence, they plot some rooty pranks,
In nature's play, they fill the blanks.

And if you listen close at night,
You'll hear their giggles, pure delight.
It's a secret world beneath your feet,
Where laughter resonates, oh so sweet.

Life's Hidden Architecture

Beneath the surface, structures rise,
With rooty beams that hold the skies.
The basil builds a leafy dome,
As tiny seeds find their sweet home.

There's tulip traffic on the main,
While radishes complain of rain.
A sturdy root is like a chair,
Where beet greens settle without a care.

The garden architect, a wise old sage,
Draws funny plans upon the page.
With leafy blueprints, roots take flight,
Constructing joy in the warm twilight.

Each turn, each twist, a funny plot,
An underground city that can't be bought.
The roots convene with dreams and schemes,
In earthy laughter, they build their dreams.

The Veil of the Undergrowth

Underneath the leafy spread,
A world awaits where laughter's bred.
With vines that twine and poke their heads,
In leafy caps, their humor spreads.

A comical contest, the roots partake,
Who can wiggle and who can shake?
With mushrooms chuckling as they cheer,
Their undergrowth games bring endless cheer.

The ferns flip-flop with such great zeal,
While daisies play an epic reel.
They dance to tunes of sun and rain,
In this secret realm, free from pain.

So next time you stroll in the sun,
Remember the roots and their funny run.
For beneath what we see, lies a mirthful trove,
Where laughter grows and joy can rove.

Harvesting Dreams from the Undergrowth

In the garden where odd thoughts grow,
I found a weed wearing a bow.
It danced around, full of delight,
Scratching its head, what a sight!

Gnomes giggled beneath the ferns,
Reading comics as the earth churns.
They said, 'Let's harvest, but wait!
Do they come in a size extra great?'

With trowels made from spoons of gold,
They dug up stories, breathtakingly bold.
'What's this?' cried one with a wink,
A root that glows and winks back in pink!

And when the sun began to sink,
The garden sparkled with dreams in sync.
So next time you wander and might,
Check your roots; they could be a delight!

Shadows of Growth.

In the corner, a shadow lies low,
Whispering secrets only plants know.
'Why did the cactus laugh at the tree?'
'Because it felt prickly, can't you see?'

Laughter swirled like leaves in the breeze,
As daisies swayed with the greatest of ease.
'Do you hear them giggle?' cried a bold sprout,
'Oh, yes,' said the soil, 'that's what it's about!'

A snail with style slid down a vine,
Wearing a hat made of dandelion.
'Grow tall, grow wide, but not too fast!'
For shadows are friends when days are past!

So gather around where giggles resound,
And let your imagination abound.
For in every plant and every seed's show,
Are shadows of laughter that bloom and grow!

Whispers from Below

Beneath the soil where whispers play,
The roots are gossiping all day.
'Did you hear about the funny worm?
He thought he could dance; oh, what a squirm!'

'The potatoes are plotting a grow-out spree,
Wearing costumes that only we can see!'
The carrots chuckled, all orange and neat,
While radishes blushed at the laughter's beat.

Up above, the flowers held their breath,
While down below, they danced until death.
'Don't let the humans in on our whim!'
'They'll try to dig us, we'll go on a limb!'

Life underground is a grand old jest,
With roots and worms, it's simply the best!
So next time you walk in the garden's flow,
Remember the giggles that whisper below!

Tangles of Time.

In the garden where vines intertwine,
Time took a twist, like aged wine.
The daisies discussed how their days are long,
While the weeds just hummed a silly song.

'Who needs a watch when you've got a bud?
Just bloom with joy; that's how it's done!'
Said one little sprig with a cheeky grin,
'It's the tangles of life where the fun begins!'

In a patch of sun where the bees had a ball,
The shadows of branches began to fall.
'What time is it?' cried the sunflowers bright,
'When you're having fun, it's always just right!'

So if you find roots that twist and tangle,
Join in the fun; don't just dangle.
For time in the garden is a riddle sublime,
And laughter is timeless in the tangles of time!

In the Depths of the Hearth

In the hearth where shadows play,
Old socks dance and laugh all day.
The cat's a king, the crumbs his throne,
While the fire crackles, we feel at home.

A potato peels itself with glee,
Juggling with a spoon, oh what a spree!
The lightbulb hums a silly tune,
As the tablecloth spins like a raccoon.

Underneath, a shoe grows roots,
As dust bunnies form their little troops.
A lost remote joins the party too,
What a wild gathering, just me and you!

So next time you peek where comfort lies,
Beneath the warmth, you'll find surprise.
With giggles and vibes that tickle your feet,
The depths of the hearth are truly sweet!

The Archive of the Ancients

Books piled high, like towers of fun,
Dusty ones whisper secrets, on the run.
With bookmarks that flutter like lost little birds,
They giggle and snicker at stale, forgotten words.

An old map crinkles, plotting a quest,
Leading to snacks that are simply the best.
Each page that turns brings a chuckling ghost,
Who drinks imaginary tea and boasts a lot most.

In the corner, a quill has lost its mind,
Writing odd verses so unrefined.
A coffee pot joins in with a giggly spout,
Spilling stories of beans that danced about.

So wander the aisles of this whimsical place,
Where laughter is scattered like glitter all over space.
You might find a dragon or two doing jigs,
In the archive of ancients, where fun never digs!

Whispers of the Wilderness

In the woods where squirrels play peek-a-boo,
Trees wear hats made of leaves, so true.
Birds gossip about last night's feast,
As the brook chuckles, saying, "I'm at least!"

A raccoon juggles acorns with flair,
While the breeze throws petals high in the air.
Mushrooms chuckle, "We're here for the show!
Join us for fun, let your silliness flow!"

The chipmunk's an artist, with twigs as his brush,
Painting the sunset in a colorful hush.
The fireflies blink in a dance so bright,
Lighting up laughter through the warm, gentle night.

In this wilderness, fun takes its flight,
Nature's a party, everything's right.
With giggles and whispers, it welcomes you dear,
To join in the revelry without any fear!

Echoes of the Past

In the attic, old echoes giggle and sway,
Chasing each other through the dust and decay.
A trunk filled with treasures, each item a tale,
Of socks that went swimming and lost their rail.

A photo spins round with a wink and a grin,
Those hairstyles! Oh goodness, where do they begin?
Grandma's old records start to play loud,
As the echoes of laughter gather a crowd.

A quilt comes alive, wrapping you tight,
With stories and patterns that twinkle at night.
The rocking chair creaks, it joins in the mirth,
Telling long stories about its old birth.

So delve into moments that twinkle and tease,
Echoes of pasts that tickle with ease.
With humor and warmth in each little nook,
You'll find giggles waiting, just take a look!

Tangled Trails of Time

In a house where the vines start to play,
I tripped on the yarns that led me astray.
My shoes got all knotted, what a sight,
Turns out I had danced with a root last night.

The clock started laughing, quite rude,
Tick-tock tickled my funky mood.
In the corners, old shoes piled high,
Trying to escape, oh my oh my!

Chairs whisper tales of a wild run,
While curtains giggle in the warm sun.
A squirrel, with a monocle, peeks inside,
Checking my strut with refined pride.

But somehow, each mishap feels just right,
Like waltzing with shadows, what a delight!
In this wacky world where giggles bloom,
I've found my joy in a tangled room.

The Roots of Reverie

In the attic where daydreams hide,
A root hat sits, in awkward pride.
It whispers tales of the past's delight,
While I juggle memories with all my might.

A blanket fort made of old shoe laces,
Creates a kingdom of silly paces.
Here, the garden gnomes plot and scheme,
Waging battles for the best sweet dream.

Oh, the dust bunnies in a pirouette,
Challenging me, how could I forget?
Among the books, a pirate reads,
While I supply the snacks, oh what deeds!

These roots, enchanted, spark a jest,
In a place where laughter feels the best.
Round and round, we dance in glee,
In a splendid realm of reverie.

Silent Stories in the Cellar

Down in the cellar, where whispers dwell,
I found a trunk full of secrets to tell.
Mice in tuxedos are twirling about,
Sipping on cheese, while they wiggle and shout.

A broomstick's solo brings quite the cheer,
As it sweeps up the dust of forgotten years.
The cobwebs twinkle like stars up high,
In this underground dance, I can't deny!

Each shadow can giggle, if you lend an ear,
As squirrels recount jokes from yesteryear.
The barrels roll laughter, you can hear it bounce,
While old socks engage in a silly prance.

With every step, a tale comes alive,
In the cellar of wonders, where spirits thrive.
I'll clink my glass with a wink and a grin,
To the silent stories that bubble within.

Vaults of Verdant Memories

Within this vault, plants twist and twine,
Each leaf a whisper, each stem a line.
They chuckle together, a leafy parade,
In the sunshine's glow, their plans are made.

A frond with glasses reads fairy tales,
While daisies create their own mail trails.
The clovers toss jokes, green as can be,
"Why did the root hide? It wanted to flee!"

Amidst all this greenery, nonsense blooms,
A cactus sidesteps, avoiding the brooms.
They all have quirks that shine through the day,
In the laughter of leaves, they tango and sway.

So here in the vaults, where the silly grows,
The fun never fades, as joy overflows.
I'll plant my heart in their giggling shoots,
In this garden of memories and hearty roots.

www.ingramcontent.com/pod-product-compliance
Lightning Source LLC
Chambersburg PA
CBHW070314120526
44590CB00017B/2666